To:
From:

THE REGINA PRESS
10 Hub Drive
Melville, New York

Edited by Julie Mitchell Marra
Artwork © Lucy Rigg

ISBN# 0-88271-046-X

Printed in Belgium.

Marriage

A Bridal Keepsake

Regina Press
New York

Dear Bride,

Love is the most beautiful gift that we can share with another. When we find that special someone whom God has chosen for us to share our lives with, we form a triangle of love with each other and God. In marriage, we share ourselves completely, as we do in our relationship with Christ.

You are about to enter into the sacrament of marriage. During this very meaningful time in your life, take time to develop your relationship with God and with each other.

Return to this little keepsake on anniversaries and birthdays and at those times when you'd like to renew the feelings that nurtured you during those wonderful days of love and anticipation. I pray this book will be a treasure as you enter into a new life with two hearts joined as one.

Julie Mitchell Marra

Our Courtship & Engagement

How we met

Our first date

When and where he proposed

What we said to each other

The first people we told

Special memories

As God's chosen ones,
holy and beloved,
clothe yourselves with compassion,
kindness, humility, meekness, and patience.
Bear with one another and,
if anyone has a complaint against another,
forgive each other;
just as the Lord has forgiven you,
so you also must forgive.
Above all,
clothe yourselves with love,
which binds everything together
in perfect harmony.
And let the peace of Christ
rule in your hearts,
to which indeed
you were called in the one body.
And be thankful.

Colossians 3:12-15

May the Lord
who loves you
bless you and your beloved
and protect you
under His wing.

May He fill each day with
moments of happiness.

And during the sad times
may you find His
reassuring, healing touch
on your lives.

May you feel His presence,
live His Word
and show His love to one another.

Beloved,
let us love one another,
because love is from God;
everyone who loves is born of God
and knows God.
Whoever does not love
does not know God,
for God is love.
God's love was revealed among us in this way:
God sent his only Son into the world
so that we might live through him.
In this is love,
not that we loved God but that he loved us
and sent his Son
to be the atoning sacrifice for our sins.
Beloved,
since God loved us so much,
we also ought to love one another.
No one has ever seen God;
if we love one another,
God lives in us,
and his love is perfected in us.

1 John 4:7-12

Grow old along with me!
The best is yet to be,
The last of life,
for which the first was made:
Our times are in his hand
Who saith,
"A whole I planned,
Youth shows but half;
trust God:
see all, nor be afraid!"

Robert Browning

I'll give my love an apple
without a core,
I'll give my love a house
without a door,
I'll give my love a palace
wherein she may be,
And she may unlock it
without any key.

My head is the apple
without a core,
My mind is the house
without a door,
My heart is the palace
wherein she maybe,
And she may unlock it
without any key.

Anonymous

My heart is like a singing bird
Whose nest is in a watered shoot:
My heart is like a rainbow shell
That paddles in a halcyon sea;
My heart is gladder than all these
Because my love is come to me.

Raise me a dais of silk and down;
Hang it with wair and purple dyes;
Carve it in doves and pomegranates,
And peacocks with a hundred eyes;
Work it in gold and silver grapes,
In leaves and silver fleurs-de-lys;
Because the birthday of my life
Is come, my love is come to me.

Christina Rossetti

Love is patient;
love is kind;
love is not envious
or boastful or arrogant or rude.
It does not insist on its own way;
it is not irritable or resentful;
it does not rejoice in wrongdoing,
but rejoices in the truth.
It bears all things,
believes all things,
hopes all things,
endures all things.
Love never ends...

1 Corinthians 13:4-8

O, my luve's like a red, red rose
That's newly sprung in June;
My luve's like the melodie
That's sweetly played in tune.

As fair thou art, my bonnie lass,
So deep in luve am I;
And I will luve thee still, my dear,
Till a' the seas gang dry.

Till all the seas gang dry, my dear,
And the rocks melt wi' the sun;
I will luve thee still, my dear,
While the sands of life shall run.

Robert Burns

Our Plans & Preparations

Our Church

Our celebrant (s)

Special marriage preparation

Day and location of bridal showers

Flowers

Music

The Rehearsal Dinner

We'll never forget

Sing to the LORD a new song,
for he has done marvelous things.
His right hand and his holy arm
have gotten him victory.
The LORD has made known his victory;
he has revealed his vindication
in the sight of the nations.
He has remembered his steadfast love
and faithfulness to the house of Israel.
All the ends of the earth
have seen the victory of our God.
Make a joyful noise to the LORD,
all the earth;
break forth into joyous song
and sing praises.

Psalm 98:1-4

How do I love thee?
Let me count the ways.
I love thee to the depth
and breadth and height
My soul can reach,
when feeling out of sight
For the ends of Being and ideal Grace.
I love thee to the level of everyday's
Most quiet need,
by sun and candle-light.
I love thee freely,
as men strive for Right;
I love thee purely,
as they turn from Praise.
I love thee with the passion put to use
In my old griefs,
and with my childhood's faith.
I love thee with a love I seemed to lose
With my lost saints,
I love thee with the breath,
Smiles, tears, of all my life!
and, if God choose,
I shall but love thee better after death.

Elizabeth Barrett Browning

The Meaning of Flowers

Apple blossoms . . . . . . better things to come
Clematis . . . . love vine
Ivy . . . . good luck
Rosebud . . . . a promise
Myrtle . . . . lover's flower
Laurel . . . . peace
Orange blossoms . . . . . fertility
Heather . . . . fortune
Baby's breath . . . . fertility
Cabbage roses . . . . richness of spirit
Anemones . . . . hope
Lily of the Valley . . . . . happiness
Red and white roses . . unity in love
Lilacs . . . . youthful love
Pansies . . . . special friendship

I will greatly rejoice in the LORD,
my whole being shall exult in my God;
for he has clothed me
with the garments of salvation,
he has covered me
with the robe of righteousness,
as a bridegroom decks himself
with a garland,
and as a bride adorns herself
with her jewels.
For as the earth brings forth its shoots,
and as a garden causes
what is sown in it to spring up,
so the Lord GOD
will cause righteousness and praise
to spring up before all the nations.

Isaiah 61:10-11

Our Wedding Day

Ceremony Date

Time

Place

Prayers

Vows

Special readings

Our wedding rings

Our reception

"For this reason
a man will leave his father and mother
and be joined to his wife,
and the two will become one flesh."
This is a great mystery,
and I am applying it
to Christ and the church.
Each of you, however,
should love his wife as himself,
and a wife should respect her husband.

Ephesians 5:31-33

Christ sanctifies
the indissoluble union
of man and woman
in mutual love and support,
to have children
and to bring them up
in the Catholic faith.

Thank you, God,
for this sacrament of marriage,
for us to be a sign of Your love
to each other and
to all people we meet.
Your love for us
is the most perfect love.
Please bless us on our marriage
and help us to lead
happy, healthy, holy lives.

My dear friends,
you have come together in this church
so that the Lord may seal
and strengthen your love
in the presence of the Church's minister
and this community.
Christ abundantly blesses this love.
He has already consecrated you in baptism
and now He enriches
and strengthens you
by a special sacrament
so that you may assume
the duties of marriage
in mutual and lasting fidelity.
And so,
in the presence of the Church,
I ask you to state your intentions.

Have you come here freely
and without reservation
to give yourselves
to each other in marriage?
Will you love and honor each other
as man and wife
for the rest of your lives?

Will you accept children
lovingly from God,
and bring them up
according to the law of Christ
and His Church?

Since it is your intention
to enter into marriage,
join your right hands,
and declare your consent
before God and His Church.

I take you to be my wife/husband,
I promise to be true to you
in good times and in bad,
in sickness and in health.
I will love you
and honor you
all the days of my life.

You have declared your consent
before the Church.
May the Lord in His goodness
strengthen your consent
and fill you both
with His blessings.
What God has joined,
men must not divide.

Dear God,

You created man and women
to be joined together
as a sign of Your covenant
with your people.
Through the sacrament of marriage,
you show us the relationship
of Christ and His Church.
We ask You
to help this couple
be a strong witness to Your love.

Bless them in their home
and bless them with children.

Grant the bride
Your help and guidance
in her role as wife and mother.
Give her Your gifts of kindness,
patience and understanding.

Grant the groom
Your help and guidance
in his role as husband and father.
Give him Your gifts of trust,
love and faithfulness.

Blessing & Exchange of Rings

May the Lord bless these rings
which you give to each other
as the sign of your love and fidelity...

Lord,
bless these rings
which we bless in Your name.
Grant that those who wear them
May always have a deep faith
in each other.
May they do your will
and always live together
in peace, good will and love.
We ask this
through Christ our Lord.

What greater thing
is there for two human souls
than to feel that
they are joined...
to strengthen each other...
to be at one with each other
in silent upspeakable memories.

George Eliot

Lord, who at Cana's wedding feast
Didst as a guest appear,
Thou dearer far than earthly guest,
Vouchsafe thy presence here;
For holy thou indeed dost prove
The marriage vow to be,
Proclaiming it a type of love
Between the Church and thee.

The holiest vow that man can make,
the golden thread of life,
The bond that none may dare to break,
That bindeth man and wife;
Which, blest by thee, whate'er betides,
No evil shall destroy,
Through anxious days each care divides,
And doubles ever joy.

On those who at thine altar kneel,
O Lord, they blessing pour,
That each may wake each other's zeal
To love thee more and more:
O grant them here in peace to live,
In purity and love,
And, this world leaving, to receive
A crown of life above. Amen.

Adelaide Thrupp, 1853
and Godfrey Thring, 1882

The love
you and your beloved feel today
is just the beginning...
focus on what God has blessed you with...
cherish the exhilarating emotions
in your life today.
These feelings
will be the foundation of your marriage.
Hold them in your heart
and pray for Almighty God
to grant your marriage
love, joy and peace forever.